THE MINIATURE BOOK OF

COFFEE

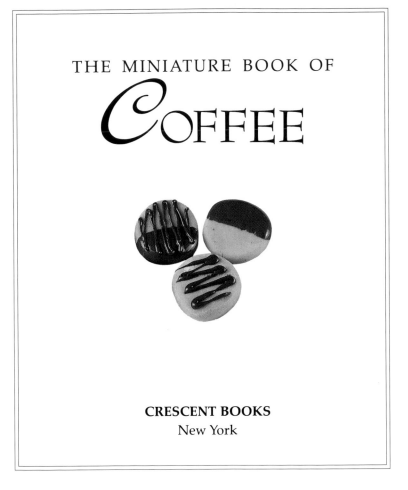

CRESCENT BOOKS
New York

Published by Salamander Books Ltd.,
129-137 York Way, London N7 9LG, United Kingdom.

© Salamander Books Ltd., 1991

This 1991 edition published by Crescent Books, distributed by
Outlet Book Company, Inc., a Random House Company,
225 Park Avenue South, New York, New York 10003.

Printed and bound in Belgium

ISBN 0-517-06542-8

8 7 6 5 4 3 2 1

CREDITS

RECIPES BY: *Caroline Cowen, Gordon Grimsdale, Carole Handslip,*
Lesley Mackley, Janice Murfitt, Lorna Rhodes and Sally Taylor

PHOTOGRAPHY BY: *Sue Atkinson, Simon Butcher, Per Ericson,*
David Gill and Paul Grater

DESIGN BY: *Tim Scott*

TYPESET BY: *Maron Graphics, Wembley*

COLOR SEPARATION BY: *P & W Graphics, Pte. Ltd.*

PRINTED IN BELGIUM BY: *Proost International Book Production,*
Turnhout, Belgium

Contents

$\mathcal{I}$CED MOCHA CHIFFON DESSERTS

4 eggs, separated
¾ cup powdered sugar, sifted
3 oz semisweet chocolate, chopped
1 tablespoon instant coffee granules
2 tablespoons water
1¼ cups whipping cream
2 tablespoons Kahlua
grated semisweet chocolate, to decorate

*T*ie a double thickness of foil around 6 ramekin dishes, to stand 1 inch above the rim of each dish. In a large bowl, beat egg yolks and powdered sugar until thick and light. In a small saucepan over a low heat, melt the chocolate in the water; stir in the coffee granules. Cool slightly, then beat into the egg yolk mixture. Whip the cream with the Kahlua; fold ¾ into chocolate mixture; chill the remainder. In a separate bowl, whip egg whites until stiff, then lightly fold into the chocolate mixture until just evenly blended. Pour into the prepared dishes and freeze 12 hours. To serve, carefully remove foil. Spoon remaining cream into a pastry bag fitted with a star nozzle, and decorate the mousses. Sprinkle with grated chocolate.
Makes 6 servings

COFFEE CARDAMOM CARAMELS

10 cardamom pods, lightly crushed
2½ cups milk
2 eggs
2 egg yolks
2 tablespoons plus 2 teaspoons superfine sugar
2 tablespoons instant coffee granules
CARAMEL:
½ cup granulated sugar
¼ cup water

*I*n a saucepan, bring the cardamom pods and milk to a boil; remove from the heat. In a heavy-bottomed saucepan, gently heat granulated sugar in the water until dissolved, then boil rapidly to a light golden brown. Pour into 6 (⅔-cup) ramekin dishes. Place the dishes in a roasting pan. In a large bowl, mix together whole eggs, egg yolks and sugar. Bring the milk almost to boiling point again, stir in coffee, then stir into the egg mixture. Strain onto the caramel in the ramekin dishes, and surround with boiling water. Place in an oven preheated to 325F (160C) until set, about 45 minutes. Remove dishes from the pan; cool then refrigerate. To serve, turn out onto individual dishes. *Makes 6 servings*

JAMAICAN COFFEE SAUCE

½ cup hot strong black coffee
2 teaspoons sugar
2 egg yolks
⅓ cup thick cream
1 teaspoon cornstarch
1 tablespoon milk
2 tablespoons dark rum

*I*n the top of a double boiler, or bowl placed over a saucepan of hot water, dissolve the sugar in the coffee. Thoroughly mix in one egg yolk at a time. Mix cornstarch with milk, stir in cream, then stir into egg yolk mixture. Cook, stirring, until thickened, 2-3 minutes. Remove from heat. Stir in rum if serving immediately. If serving cold, let sauce cool, stirring occasionally, and add rum just before serving. *Makes about 1 cup*

NOTE: As a variation, you can add coffee-flavored liqueur in place of the rum.

COFFEE MOUSSES

¼ cup butter
3 tablespoons light corn syrup
2 cups vanilla wafer crumbs
⅔ cup whipping cream, whipped, and liqueur
coffee beans to decorate
3 tablespoons cornstarch
¼ cup superfine sugar
1 tablespoon instant coffee granules
1¼ cups milk
2 eggs, separated
1 tablespoon plus 2 teaspoons plain gelatin
dissolved in 3 tablespoons hot water
1¼ cups whipping cream, whipped

*I*n a saucepan, melt butter and corn syrup; mix in cookie crumbs. Divide between 8 plastic wrap-lined molds, pressing evenly. Refrigerate. In a saucepan, mix cornstarch, sugar, coffee and milk, bring to a boil, stirring, and cook 2 minutes. Off the heat, beat in egg yolks. Slowly stir gelatin into coffee mixture. Let stand until thick. Fold in cream. In a bowl, whip egg whites until stiff, then fold in. Fill molds, cover and refrigerate. To serve, turn out onto plates; remove plastic wrap. Decorate with whipped cream and coffee beans. *Makes 8 servings*

$\mathcal{M}$OCHA FONDUE

8 oz dark chocolate, chopped
3 teaspoons instant coffee powder
3 tablespoons Tia Maria
⅔ cup thick cream
A selection of fresh fruit, to serve

NUTTY MERINGUES:

2 egg whites
½ cup superfine sugar
2 oz flaked almonds, lightly toasted

For the nutty meringues, in a bowl, whip egg whites until stiff, fold in ⅓ sugar, whisk again until stiff then lightly fold in remaining sugar. Place teaspoonsful on baking sheets lined with non-stick paper; insert a few almonds in each. Bake in an oven preheated to 110C (225F) until crisp and dry, about 1½-2 hours. Turn off oven; leave meringues in oven to cool. Peel cooled meringues off paper.

For the fondue, in a fondue pot, gently heat chocolate, coffee, Tia Maria and cream, stirring, until smooth. Keep warm over burner, and serve with almond meringues and fresh fruit. *Makes 6 servings*

$\mathcal{M}$OCHA SAUCE

1 tablespoon dark very strong coarsely ground expresso coffee
1¼ cups whipping cream
3 oz semisweet chocolate, chopped
1½ teaspoons butter

*I*n a saucepan, bring coffee and whipping cream to a boil, remove from heat and let stand 30 minutes. Place chocolate in top of a double boiler or a bowl. Strain in creamy coffee. Place over a pan of simmering water and stir until chocolate melts. Whisk in butter until smooth. Serve at once. *Makes 6-8 servings*

NOTE: Serve hot with Coffee Bombe, page 20, or poached pears, ice cream or souffles, if desired.

COFFEE BOMBE

3 eggs, separated
¾ cup superfine sugar
1⅓ cups cold strong coffee
2 cups whipping cream, whipped
5 oz meringues, crushed
Mocha Sauce, page 18, to serve
whipped cream and chocolate coffee beans to decorate

*L*ightly oil a 4-cup bombe mold. In a large bowl, beat egg yolks and sugar until light. Gently stir in coffee, cream and meringues. In a medium-size bowl, whisk egg whites until stiff. Fold 1 tablespoon into coffee mixture, then carefully fold coffee mixture into egg whites. Pour into an oiled 4-cup bombe mold; freeze until firm. To serve, place bombe in refrigerator 1 hour to soften slightly. Turn out onto a serving dish, decorate with whipped cream and chocolate coffee beans. Serve with hot sauce. *Makes 8 servings*

RICH PECAN CAKE

¾ cup light-brown sugar
4 egg yolks
1⅓ cups pecans, ground
1 tablespoon dried white bread crumbs
1 tablespoon strong coffee
3 egg whites
1¼ cups whipping cream
1 tablespoon strong coffee
3-4 tablespoons maple syrup
2 (1 oz) squares semisweet chocolate, melted
8 rose leaves

*I*n a bowl, beat sugar and egg yolks until light. Gently fold in nuts and bread crumbs, then stir in coffee. In a bowl, whisk egg whites until soft peaks form; fold into mixture. Pour into pan and bake in an oven pre-heated to 350F (175C) until well risen and firm to touch, 25-30 minutes. Cool on a wire rack. To make chocolate leaves, brush chocolate over underside of rose leaves. Place on waxed paper; let stand until set; peel off leaves. For the filling, in a bowl, whip cream and coffee until thick; stir in maple syrup. Slice cake horizontally in 2 and sandwich together with ½ cream. Spread remaining cream over cake and decorate with chocolate leaves. *Makes 8 servings*

ALMOND MOCHA CAKE

6 oz semisweet chocolate, chopped
¼ cup cold coffee
12 tablespoons unsalted butter, softened
1 cup packed dark-brown sugar
4 eggs, separated
1⅓ cups ground almonds
½ cup all-purpose flour, sifted
1½ cups powdered sugar, sifted
1 tablespoon coffee extract
water
8 chocolate-coated nuts, to decorate

*I*n a small saucepan, gently melt chocolate in coffee. In a large bowl, beat butter and brown sugar until light. Beat in 1 egg yolk at a time, then beat in warm chocolate. Fold in ground almonds and flour. In a bowl, beat egg whites until fairly stiff. Fold 2 tablespoons into chocolate mixture then gently fold in remainder. Spoon into a greased and lined deep 8-inch round cake pan and bake in an oven preheated to 325F (165C) 1-1¼ hours. Cool on a wire rack. For the icing, in a small bowl, place sugar. Stir in coffee extract and enough water to make a thick consistency. Coat cake top and side completely. Decorate with chocolate-coated nuts. *Makes 8 servings*

$\mathcal{I}$TALIAN COFFEE LAYER CAKE

3 eggs
½ cup plus 1 tablespoon superfine sugar
¾ cup all-purpose flour
1 tablespoon instant coffee granules
12 oz mascarpone cheese
4 egg yolks
½ cup superfine sugar
2 tablespoons rum
2 egg whites, stiffly whisked
¾ cup coffee
2 (1 oz) squares semisweet chocolate, grated

*F*or the cake, in a bowl, beat eggs and sugar until light. Gently fold in flour and coffee granules. Spoon into a deep 8-inch round cake pan lined with waxed paper and bake in an oven preheated to 350F (175C) until golden, 30 minutes. Cool on a wire rack. For the filling, in a bowl, beat mascarpone until soft. In another bowl, beat egg yolks and sugar until light. Stir in mascarpone and rum. Fold egg whites into cheese mixture. Cut cake horizontally in 3 layers. Put 1 layer on a serving plate. Sprinkle with ⅓ of coffee. Cover with ⅓ of filling. Repeat layers, finishing with cheese mixture. Refrigerate overnight. Sprinkle with grated chocolate. *Makes 8 servings*

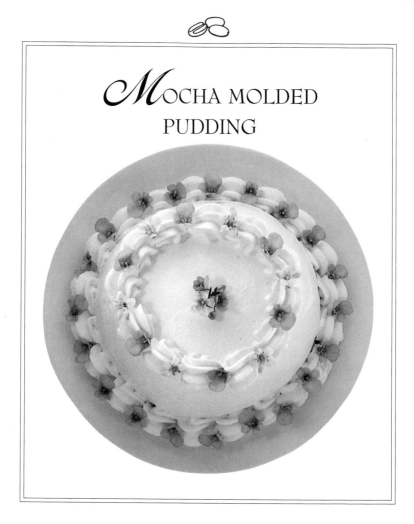

$\mathcal{M}$OCHA MOLDED
PUDDING

9 oz semisweet chocolate, chopped
¼ cup plus 1 tablespoon strong coffee
12 tablespoons unsalted butter, diced
¾ cup superfine sugar
4 large eggs, beaten
1½ cups whipping cream, whipped
tiny edible flowers to decorate, if desired

*I*n the top of a double boiler, or a bowl set over a pan of simmering water, melt chocolate in coffee, stirring until smooth. Gradually beat in butter and sugar until butter has melted. Off the heat, gradually beat in eggs. Strain into a 4-cup bowl or souffle dish lined with a double thickness of foil, placed in a roasting pan. Surround dish with boiling water and bake in an oven preheated to 350F (175C) until there is a thick crust on top, about 1 hour. Cool, then refrigerate. To serve, turn out onto a serving dish and carefully peel away foil. Cover pudding with ⅔ of the whipped cream. Pipe remaining cream around pudding and decorate with flowers, if desired. *Makes 6-8 servings*

$\mathscr{P}$ECAN PIE

1½ cups all-purpose flour
¼ cup plus 3 tablespoons unsalted butter
1 tablespoon superfine sugar
1 egg yolk beaten with 1 tablespoon water
⅔ cup maple syrup
½ cup light-brown sugar
3 eggs
2 tablespoons instant coffee granules dissolved in
1 tablespoon hot milk
1½ cups pecans
whipped cream or vanilla ice cream, to serve, if desired

*F*or the pastry, sift flour into a bowl. Cut in butter until mixture resembles bread crumbs, then stir in sugar followed by beaten egg yolk. Knead lightly to a firm dough. Cover and refrigerate 30 minutes. On a lightly floured surface, roll out pastry and line an 8-inch pie pan. For the filling, in a saucepan, heat maple syrup and brown sugar until sugar has dissolved; cool slightly. In a bowl, beat eggs and coffee-flavored milk; stir in maple syrup mixture and pecans. Pour into prepared pan and bake in an oven preheated to 375F (190C) until filling has set, 30-40 minutes. Serve warm or cold with whipped cream or vanilla ice cream, if desired. *Makes 6-8 servings*

COFFEE ALMOND SHORTCAKE

2 cups all-purpose flour
2 tablespoons unsalted butter
$\frac{1}{2}$ cup superfine sugar
$\frac{2}{3}$ cup ground almonds
$\frac{1}{3}$ cup superfine sugar
$\frac{1}{2}$ cup powdered sugar
1 egg yolk
2 teaspoons strong coffee
about 2 tablespoons blanched almonds to decorate

*P*reheat oven to 325F (160C). Butter a 9-inch loose-bottomed pie pan. For the shortbread, sift flour into a bowl. Cut in butter, then stir in superfine sugar. Knead to firm dough. For the marzipan, in a bowl, mix ground almonds and sugar. Stir in egg yolk and coffee, to make a firm mixture. On a lightly floured surface, roll out to a circle slightly smaller than diameter of prepared pan. Divide shortbread in 2 portions, 1 slightly larger than the other. Roll out larger piece and press over bottom and side of pan. Lay marzipan on top. Roll out second piece of shortbread to fit pan and place on top of marzipan; press firmly together around edge. Press almonds on top. Bake in oven 45-50 minutes or until golden-brown and firm. Cool in pan; remove. To serve cut in wedges. *Makes 6-8 servings*

COFFEE & CARAWAY ROLLS

3 cups bread flour
1 teaspoon salt
⅔ (¼ oz) pkg fast-rising yeast (2 teaspoons)
2 teaspoons caraway seeds
¼ cup butter
¾ cup milk
2 tablespoons instant coffee granules
1 teaspoon superfine sugar
1 egg, beaten
1 teaspoon caraway seeds

*G*rease a baking sheet. Sift flour and salt into a bowl. Stir in yeast and caraway seeds. In a small saucepan, gently heat butter, milk and coffee to 125F-130F (50C-55C). Stir in sugar to dissolve. Form well in center of flour, pour in liquid ingredients and mix thoroughly. Knead well until smooth and elastic. Put in a large bowl, cover loosely with plastic wrap and let stand to rise, about 2 hours. Knead lightly on floured surface 2-3 minutes. Divide in 8. Roll each piece in a thin "sausage" and knot in center. Place on greased baking sheet. Cover and let rise 45 minutes. Brush with beaten egg and sprinkle with caraway seeds. Bake in an oven preheated to 400F (205C) 15-20 minutes. *Makes 8 rolls*

$\mathcal{C}$OFFEE PALMIERS

8 oz puff pastry
superfine sugar for dredging
¼ cup superfine sugar
1 tablespoon instant coffee granules

*O*n a surface dredged with superfine sugar, roll out pastry to a 12- × 8-inch rectangle. In a bowl, mix ¼ cup superfine sugar and coffee granules. Sprinkle ½ of mixture over pastry. Fold long edges of pastry into middle, then fold long sides together. On sugared surface, roll out pastry to same size rectangle. Sprinkle with remaining sugar and coffee mixture. Fold long edges into middle; fold into middle again, then press together with a rolling pin. Cut dough in ½-inch pieces. Place on baking sheets, allowing room to spread slightly. Bake in an oven, pre-heated to 375F (190C) 15-20 minutes, until crisp and golden, turning over halfway through baking. Cool on wire racks.
Makes 30 pieces

COFFEE CREAMS

2 cups granulated sugar
²/₃ cup water
pinch of cream of tartar
3 tablespoons half and half
½ teaspoon strong coffee
3 (1 oz) squares semisweet chocolate, melted
walnut halves, if desired

*I*n a heavy saucepan, gently dissolve the sugar in the water, stirring. Bring to a boil, add the cream of tartar and boil to 240F (116C); a few drops of syrup will form a soft ball when dropped into a cup of cold water. Stir in half and half. Pour onto a work surface sprinkled with a little cold water. Let stand until a skin forms around the edges, then, using a spatula and working in a figure-8 movement, turn the mixture until it becomes thick, opaque and grainy; knead in coffee. Form pieces the size of a small walnut into balls, then press to flatten. Let stand overnight. Either dip 1 half of each fondant in melted chocolate and place on waxed paper to set or drizzle melted chocolate on the tops. Decorate with walnuts, if desired. *Makes 20 pieces*

COFFEE TRUFFLES

CHOCOLATE CUPS:
5 (1 oz) squares semisweet chocolate, chopped
1 teaspoon sunflower oil
FILLING:
⅔ cup whipping cream
1 tablespoon instant coffee granules
6 (1 oz) squares white chocolate, chopped
2 teaspoons brandy

For the chocolate cups, in a bowl placed over a saucepan of hot water, melt the chocolate in the oil, stirring until smooth. Spread evenly over the inside of 20 double thickness petit four cups. Refrigerate to set. Remelt chocolate, if necessary, to spread a second layer of chocolate in cups. Refrigerate to set; carefully peel off paper cups.

For the filling, in a saucepan, bring cream and coffee to a boil, stirring until coffee has dissolved. Off the heat, stir in the chocolate until melted. Over a low heat, stir until mixture begins to bubble; cool. Beat in brandy until thick. Spoon into a pastry bag fitted with a large star nozzle and pipe into chocolate cups. Store in refrigerator; eat within 2-3 days. *Makes 20 pieces*

COFFEE COCKTAILS

CAFÉ ALEXANDER

crushed ice
2 tablespoons strong coffee, chilled and sweetened to taste
2 tablespoons crème de cacao
2 tablespoons plus 2 teaspoons brandy
2 tablespoons whipping cream, chilled
chocolate curls, to decorate

*I*n a cocktail shaker, shake crushed ice, coffee, crème de cacao, brandy and cream until well mixed. Strain into a glass. Decorate with chocolate curls. *Makes 1 serving*

IRISH COFFEE

1 teaspoon light-brown sugar
2 tablespoons Irish Whiskey
½ cup hot freshly made coffee
2 tablespoons whipping cream

*P*ut sugar, whiskey and coffee into a heatproof glass. Dip a teaspoon into coffee to warm it, then carefully pour cream over back of spoon to float on coffee. For *Jamaican Coffee*, replace Irish Whiskey with dark Rum and sprinkle cream with grated nutmeg. *Makes 1 serving*

COFFEE COCKTAILS

CAFÉ BRÛLOT

4 cloves
strip of lemon and orange peel
½ cinnamon stick
1 tablespoon light-brown sugar
¼ cup brandy
2 cups hot freshly made coffee

*I*n a bowl, put cloves, lemon and orange peel, cinnamon and sugar. In a ladle, warm brandy; light and pour into bowl. Stir until sugar has dissolved. Slowly stir in coffee. Ladle into warmed cups. For *Café de Olla*, replace citrus peel and brandy with 1 (2-inch) cinnamon stick. *Makes 4 servings*

ALMOND COFFEE

1 teaspoon light-brown sugar
2 tablespoons amaretto liqueur
½ cup hot freshly made coffee
whipped cream and slivered almonds, toasted

*P*ut sugar, Amaretto and coffee into a heatproof glass. Stir together, top with whipped cream and sprinkle with almonds. *Makes 1 serving*